Original title:
Dewdrops and Daydreams

Author: Nora Sinclair

ISBN HARDBACK: 978-1-80566-617-2
ISBN PAPERBACK: 978-1-80566-902-9

Moonlit Drizzles of Imagined Skies

Under a disco ball of light,
I dance with shadows in the night.
A squirrel in a tux, oh what a sight,
Who knew the stars would invite a fright?

The clouds play silly hide-and-seek,
As giggles echo, playful and meek.
A jester moon with a painted cheek,
Whispers secrets, as if to speak.

Secrets Beneath the Morning Grass

The ants throw a party underneath,
In the morning's dew, they find their feast.
With tiny hats and crumbs to eat,
They shimmy about with a rhythm, neat.

A ladybug sings a silly song,
While the grasshoppers just hop along.
With petals dance like a fairy throng,
Nature's stage, where everyone belongs.

Dreamscapes Awash in Tender Glow

A marshmallow cloud drifts with a grin,
Where gummy bears play, and giggles begin.
The sun, a clown with a pie on its chin,
Spills jelly beans where the laughter spins.

Fluffy kittens float on cotton candy,
While rainbows leap, bright and dandy.
A cupcake army, tasty and handy,
Is ready to march, sweet and randy.

Echoes of the Twilight Breeze

The wind whispers tales of possibility,
As butterflies sashay with agility.
The crickets compose symphonies of glee,
While fireflies twinkle in their own jubilee.

A hedgehog wearing glasses reads a book,
With every turn, a mischievous look.
In the twilight, laughter is the hook,
Where dreams bounce around like a playful crook.

Embraces of Silent Whispers

A sneeze in the dawn, a giggle of light,
The sun trips over shadows, a silly sight.
A flower yawned wide, fell flat on the grass,
It tickled the bee who then muttered, "Alas!"

The breeze chuckled softly, a gentle jest,
As butterflies danced in a comical quest.
A leaf tried to jive, but it lost its step,
While ants held a meeting, in a haphazard prep.

Murmurs in the Heart of Bloom

A daffodil quipped, “I’m too bright today!”
While daisies giggled, in their own little fray.
The tulips donned shades, made quite the scene,
As they pranced in the garden, so carefree and green.

A worm shared a joke, in the soil so deep,
But the rose rolled its eyes, then fell back to sleep.
A bug with a tie said, “I’m off to a show!”
While the petals exchanged tales of the day’s fashion flow.

In the Theater of the Morning Sky

Clouds played tag, with a wink and a smile,
While the sun donned a hat, in a charming style.
A star slipped and stumbled, fell right out of place,
And the moon burst out laughing, “What’s with your face?”

The sky held a party, balloons made of light,
With rainbows providing the dance floor so bright.
A comet brought cake, with sprinkles galore,
While planets teamed up for a game of charades, sure!

Glances of Infinity in a Tear

A raindrop rolled down, with a comical sigh,
“Life’s just a splash, don’t be shy, oh my!”
It landed on roses, who giggled with glee,
“Let’s put on a show, for all to see!”

The puddles reflected, a circus of fun,
Where frogs wore top hats, jumping one by one.
A snail made a splash, in a very slow race,
While the thunder chuckled, adding to the space.

Whispers of Morning Mist

A squirrel in pajamas, it struts with flair,
Chasing sunlight, without a single care.
The world is a circus, topsy-turvy and loud,
As raindrops giggle beneath a fluffy cloud.

Coffee cups dance, spilling tales in the air,
While toast keeps teasing, a crispy affair.
The cat wears a crown of spaghetti and cheese,
Purring softly while plotting to seize the breeze.

Silhouettes of Sunlight

Shadows play tag with a wandering bee,
While grass blades wiggle, all jolly and free.
A hats-off to rabbits who jump with a wink,
In the garden of mischief, where giggles all sync.

The sun pulls a prank, hides behind a tree,
Leaving puddles of laughter by the old bumblebee.
Socks on the line wave like hands in the air,
Cheering the chaos with joy beyond compare.

Ribbons of Clouded Thoughts

Clouds wear bow ties and float with style,
While a bird on a branch serenades with a smile.
Thoughts tumble like marbles, all rollicking round,
As the wind cracks a joke with a whimsical sound.

An octopus juggles while riding a bike,
In a show of wonders, broadly unlike.
Umbrellas do tango, twirling in delight,
As the sun sets the stage for a fabulous night.

Tides of Tranquil Reflection

Waves whisper secrets to a sleepy old log,
As fish don their party hats, making a slog.
A tire swing giggles, riding the breeze,
While frogs croak their tunes with the utmost ease.

The moon spins around, a disco ball bright,
Sending waves to boogie, twirling in flight.
Splashing in puddles of shimmering glee,
What a wacky world, come join the spree!

The Breath of Possibility in New Beginnings

Awake with a giggle, the sun starts to peek,
A cat in a tutu, oh what a cheek!
The toast is a dancer, the coffee a clown,
While socks on the floor wear a mysterious frown.

A spoon does the cha-cha, a fork strikes a pose,
The fridge hums a melody, everybody knows.
With cereal confetti and milk that can sing,
Today’s a wild party, let’s give it a swing.

Shards of Magic in the Morning Air

A squirrel in a hat, or maybe it's bright,
Plans for today keep popping in sight.
A biscuit does ballet, the jam jumps for joy,
And toast flips a pancake, oh what a ploy!

The kettle starts whistling, it's laughter and cheer,
It's a circus of flavors, oh bring them all near!
With muffins like mountains and pancakes like dreams,
Life is a jester, bursting with schemes.

Echoes of Yesterday in Today's Glare

The cat has a theory about time-traveling mice,
She claims they steal snacks, but she's not too precise.
Yesterday's memories in shades of bright fun,
The dog tells a tale of a race that he won.

You'd laugh at the antics of socks that go rogue,
They wander and tumble, like an adventurous vogue.
With leftovers conspiring, the pot spins a yarn,
In this world of nonsense, who needs a barn?

Luminous Threads Connecting Dreams

The moon wears pajamas, so cozy and wide,
While stars in a line have a conga-line ride.
Clouds play peek-a-boo with a glimmering wink,
And thoughts float like bubbles, just waiting to link.

The day mingles softly with giggles and cheer,
And wishes on stars make the evening sincere.
With laughter like ribbons that dance in the breeze,
Life’s a sweet whisper that tickles with ease.

Veils of Silvered Rain

Tiny pearls hang from each leaf,
A fashion show, nature's sneaky thief.
They glisten and shimmer, such a sight,
Even snails can strut in morning light.

Bouncing on rooftops, they make a song,
A splash of giggles where they belong.
Wiggly worms dance, thinking they’re cool,
While raindrops play tag, breaking every rule.

Mornings Wrapped in Light

Sunbeams peek through the curtains wide,
Chasing sleep like a playful tide.
Caffeinated shadows prance and tease,
While toast pops up with a crispy breeze.

Socks mismatched, a fashion faux pas,
Tangled in laughter, they giggle ha ha.
The cat takes a leap, then slides with grace,
Chasing her tail in a bright, warm embrace.

Secrets Beneath the Veil of Fog

Cloudy wisps play hide and seek,
Muffled secrets, whispers they peak.
The trees dressed up in ghostly gowns,
Epic parties without any clowns.

Fog completes his famous dance,
Funny antics, a silly romance.
Cars honk, thinking they've lost their way,
While the fog bows out, just for a sway.

Floating on a Sea of Reflections

Puddles mirror a quirky world,
Where frogs wear crowns and petals twirled.
A fish takes a selfie with a duck,
And both agree it's pure luck!

Ripples giggle, the wind takes flight,
As shadows join the playful night.
The moon grins down with a wink and sigh,
While stars play hopscotch across the sky.

Wandering through Soft Morning Hues

In the light of soft dawn's tease,
A squirrel dances with the breeze.
Chasing shadows, a silly parade,
While the sun yawns, unafraid.

Pancakes flip and birds take flight,
A penguin waddles, what a sight!
Clouds wearing hats, oh what a flair,
Morning giggles fill the air.

Butterflies sip on nectar's bliss,
A bee just buzzed his morning kiss.
With petals quaking in laughter's wake,
Who knew mornings could be this fake?

So, join the frolic, frothy and bright,
In this playful dance of light.
For every giggle and silly tease,
Mornings burst like ripe, sweet peas.

A Tapestry of Gentle Mornings

Morning's quilt is stitched with cheer,
As toast pops up, oh, what a year!
Jam on fingers, sticky and sweet,
Who needs coffee? This is a treat!

The cat's in a hat, a purring delight,
Socks on the dog, what a funny sight!
A chorus of roosters clucks in a row,
Making breakfast a lively show!

Pigeons prance in their feathered suits,
While children giggle in brightly colored boots.
World awakens with a silly grin,
As we dive into fun, let the day begin!

With each tickle of morning's kiss,
A sneaky breeze brings pure bliss.
Sailing on laughter, joyous and free,
Every moment's a gift, don't you agree?

Reflections in the Crystal Veil

Splashing water, a frog with flair,
Kangaroos bouncing without a care.
A mirror of giggles in shimmering streams,
Nature whispers its silliest dreams.

A fish wearing glasses, oh what a thing,
Sings silly songs, making bubbles sing.
The pond is a stage with frogs as the stars,
While bugs play drums on their tiny guitars!

Ripples dance like they've had a sip,
Ducks are twirling, doing a flip.
With laughter echoing through leafy lanes,
Morning mischief is where joy reigns!

Reflecting fun in every small wave,
Nature's circus, so wild and brave.
Join the madness, let worries melt,
In this crystal veil, pure joy is felt.

Enchanted Threads of Gossamer Air

A spider spins with great delight,
Crafting webs that shimmer bright.
With threads of laughter gently spun,
Every breeze sends giggles on the run.

A butterfly, with a monocle style,
Surveys the scene with a charming smile.
Laughter bubbles like a spring-fed brook,
As the morning's magic, we now took.

Twirling dandelion seeds in the sky,
Join the parade as they float by.
The air is thick with chattery fun,
Tugging on smiles as bright as the sun!

With every whisper of gentle air,
Silly thoughts dance without a care.
Embrace the magic, let joy ensnare,
In this enchanted world, love is everywhere!

The Kaleidoscope of Awakening Thoughts

A squirrel in a suit, what a sight,
He juggles acorns with all his might.
A dance of shadows beneath the tree,
Who knew such antics could bring such glee?

The sun winks at the ladybugs' race,
As they zoom around in a frenetic chase.
With each tiny hop, they giggle and cheer,
Making flowers blush in the warm atmosphere.

A butterfly dons a cape, flying high,
While a snail with a hat just can't tell why.
In every odd nook, a chuckle is found,
Turning the usual into joy all around.

Spheres of Light in Quiet Places

The lamp post tells tales of old street fights,
With pigeons, the champions, catching the sights.
A moonbeam slips through to tickle a cat,
Making it jump and land flat on a mat.

A chipmunk in glasses reads tales with glee,
While a butterfly sneezes, buzzing with spree.
In a maze of daisies, the fairies all play,
Turning the mundane into a carnival display.

The wind starts to giggle, rustling the leaves,
As they dance together, just like old thieves.
Each corner whispers a curious jest,
Transforming the quiet into a lively fest.

A Horizon Awash with Fantasy

A cloud looks like candy, floating just right,
While shadows of giants leap into the light.
Fish wear tiny hats, just swimming along,
Their scales shine like laughter, a jubilant song.

The grass tickles toes with a playful tease,
As daisies throw parties, inviting the bees.
A turtle races a rabbit, both start to grin,
The finish line's drawn with a wild spin.

Stars play hide and seek with the moon's soft glow,
While the night sprinkles laughter, a wondrous show.
Whimsical wonders reveal every quirk,
Turning routine moments into pure work.

Glints of Reflection in Every Shadow

A puddle winks back at the leaps of the frogs,
As shadows make faces while stretching like dogs.
A ladybug laughs so loud, it’s absurd,
Trying to catch wisps of the wind with a word.

Chasing their tails, the shadows all play,
Tickling the ground in a comical way.
The flick of an ear sends echoes of cheer,
While the sun plays peek-a-boo, hiding from fear.

A chessboard of ants in a silly parade,
Each move's a delight, a perfect charade.
In every reflection, the humor is found,
Transforming the ordinary into laughter profound.

Threads of Twilight's Embrace

In the evening light they play,
A spider's web on display.
Glow worms having a dance-off,
While the moon begins to scoff.

With crickets chirping silly tunes,
And raccoons wearing hats like loons.
The stars giggle up above,
As shadows flirt with dreams of love.

Fluffy clouds like cotton candy,
As fireflies buzz, oh so dandy.
The night wears laughter in its folds,
With secrets only twilight holds.

So join the fun, don’t be late,
For twilight weaves a funny fate.
In every corner, chuckles hide,
In this playful world, we’ll abide.

Serene Portraits of Dawn

Morning breaks with giggles bright,
Sunlight tickles with delight.
Birds wear ties, all ready to sing,
As squirrels perform their acorn fling.

Pajama-clad sunflowers cheer,
While bees buzz in a playful sphere.
The coffee pot dances a jig,
As laughter fills the air, quite big.

A canvas painted with bright hues,
While roosters prance in silly shoes.
The world awakens, vibrant, fun,
As dewy grass becomes the run.

So take a sip of morning's treat,
And join the joyful, hectic beat.
For dawn arrives with whimsy grand,
And tickles all across the land.

Dancing Shadows on Blossoms

Shadows skippin' like they're spry,
On flowers looking up to sky.
The lilacs laugh, oh what a sight,
As butterflies join in the flight.

The sun slips on its goofy hat,
While daisies bounce, how about that?
Hummingbirds play hide and seek,
In this garden, joy's not meek.

With petals twirling in the breeze,
Frogs are croaking silly sneeze.
The tulips join a conga line,
In this patch where all things shine.

So swing along with nature's tune,
Dance with the shadows, oh so soon.
In this garden, laughter grows,
As every creature shares their prose.

Traces of a Dreamer's Path

Footprints in the sand are spry,
With giggles trailing as they fly.
A path of whims, quite round and twisty,
With surprises that are bound to misty.

Stars that giggle and little moons,
Winking down with silly tunes.
The dreamer's hat lost in the chase,
Chasing laughter all over the place.

Clouds wear spectacles, oh so wise,
As dreamers chase their wise goodbyes.
In lands where pillow fights reside,
And every turn is full of pride.

So follow paths where laughter flows,
In this world where whimsy grows.
Each step a jest, each breath a cheer,
As dreams ignite, loud and clear.

Secrets Unraveled in the Morning Glow

A squirrel in a bowtie, so smart,
Planning a heist with a breakfast tart.
He dances on roofs, with flair and grace,
While robins critique from their lofty place.

The cat makes a claim on the sunny spot,
Pretending to hunt for the world's last thought.
With one well-placed leap, it's a comedy scene,
As she lands in the dog's nap, quite unforeseen!

A pancake flops down from a chimney's top,
The neighbors all gasp, should they call a cop?
But no, it’s just breakfast, an aerial treat,
As pancakes aim to land on my street, oh sweet!

So here in the morn, we chuckle and cheer,
For secrets unfold with a side of good cheer.
Each laughter a sprinkle, each giggle a ray,
In the brightening hour of this silly new day.

Luminous Reflections of a Dreaming Heart

The muffin was glowing, a sight to behold,
Telling its story, a tale to be told.
It sang of the baker who added too much,
With frosting that sparkled, oh, what a touch!

A pancake parade in the kitchen today,
That's right, they march in a syrupy way.
The spatula leads with a flourish so grand,
As the toaster plays trumpet, it’s quite the band!

A cat in a chef's hat, what’s this newfound trend?
Whisking up chaos, can anyone tend?
With a sprinkle of laughter, he flips pancakes high,
While the dog rolls his eyes with a big, heavy sigh.

And thus, in this morning, our laughter takes flight,
A sweet, silly journey that starts with the light.
With yumminess swirling and fun in the air,
We welcome the bright day, no problem, just flair!

Wistful Breezes of a New Dawn

An owl with a monocle studies the scene,
As chickens all plot in the bright morning sheen.
They cluck about secrets that roosters might share,
While trying to decide who should first get the fare.

The wind whips through flowers with a giggle and tug,
Tickling their petals, giving each stem a hug.
Rabbits do a jig with an awkward two-step,
As daisies all cheer, betting he'll lose his rep!

A lazy bee buzzes, still stuck in a dream,
He orders some nectar from an urgent ice cream.
With sprinkles of sunshine, he dances about,
While ladybugs giggle, it's a sunny route out!

So relish the morn, let the laughter unfold,
For whimsy and joy, together we hold.
Each breeze whispers softly, while tickling the grass,
Inviting us all to just let moments pass.

Fragments of Light in a Sea of Quiet

A butterfly dons her best polka dot dress,
Teasing a snail who's a little bit stressed.
They giggle and tease as they dance on the ground,
While a jumpy grasshopper looks on, then rebounds!

Morning brings giggles from a nearby brook,
Where frogs wear sunglasses, just take a look!
Each splash is a joke, each ribbit a prank,
As turtles salute from their sunbathing flank.

A gust gives a nudge to an old rusted swing,
Where dreams are remembered and laughter takes wing.
Birds holler with joy, a cacophony bright,
While owls sleep on, dreaming late into night.

So gather the fragments, this moment, so rare,
In a quiet sea of fun, feel the air.
Each chuckle, a ripple in life's playful quest,
With light-hearted whispers that bring out the best.

Plumes of Hope in Stillness

In puddles of light, they dance and prance,
Tickling the grass, a whimsical chance.
A butterfly sneezes, oh what a show,
As ants in a line form a funny tableau.

A snail on a mission, moving so slow,
Waving at flowers, putting on a show.
A rabbit's quick hop, a froggy retreat,
As they slip on the dew, what a slippery feat!

Breezes that whisper of mischief’s delight,
Chasing the shadows ’til the fall of night.
With giggles entwined in nature’s embrace,
The world spins around in a topsy-turvy race.

And when the sun sets, we laugh with a cheer,
For all the odd moments that keep us near.
With plumes of sweet hope, we revel and boast,
In nature's weird wonders, we’ll always toast.

Caresses of Twilight's Glow

As stars wink above in the inky night,
The moon cracks a joke, oh what a sight!
Fireflies twinkle like living confetti,
While toads croak their puns, oh so steady.

In corners of gardens, a laugh blooms anew,
A gopher in glasses is reading the news.
The breeze tickles branches, makes them sway,
As laughter spills out, brightening the gray.

A cat with a swagger, oh what a tease,
Prowls with a purpose, up high in the trees.
With paws on the branch, he suddenly slips,
And lands in a bush, now sporting some quips!

As twilight caresses with laughter's sweet grace,
We'll chuckle and chortle, each funny face.
In this magical hour, mischief's a friend,
As the day turns to night, and the laughter won't end.

Horizon’s Breath in Still Waters

The pond’s like a mirror, reflecting the sky,
Where ducks wear top hats, oh my, oh my!
A turtle in shades, lounging on a rock,
Complains about sunburn—what a funny shock!

As lily pads giggle and croak with delight,
The fish play a game of hide and take flight.
With splashes of joy, they leap high and spin,
Making ripples of laughter, let the fun begin!

A dragonfly buzzing, a fly on a spree,
Runs into a frog, “Hey, watch where you flee!”
They chuckle and tumble, a slippery show,
A banquet of giggles in the water below.

In stillness, we find the humor of life,
Through quips and quick jests, joy’s never rife.
As the horizon breathes, we relish the play,
In the splashes of laughter, we’ll always stay.

The Language of Sighing Ferns

In forests of ferns, with a whisper, they speak,
Of secrets and tales from the funny and meek.
A squirrel with sass sings a tune in a tree,
While mice hold a meeting on who's next to flee!

In puddles of giggles, a hedgehog will trot,
Wearing a crown made of leaves, quite the plot!
As fireflies join in, they light up the gloom,
Turning this chatter into a party room.

"Did you hear what the owl hooted last night?"
"It's ruffling feathers, oh what a fright!"
Echoes of laughter spread wide through the glen,
While ferns sway in time to this jolly refrain.

With nature as witness, we dance and we play,
In the language of sighs, we chase woes away.
As stories unfold beneath boughs that twist,
Life's hilarious moments are too sweet to miss.

Flickers of Imagination at Daybreak

A squirrel wears a tiny hat,
Dancing on the fence post, fat.
The sun peeks through with a grin,
Laughing at where dreams begin.

A breeze tells jokes with a sigh,
As clouds go drifting, oh my my!
The flowers giggle, swaying wide,
While sleepy bugs dance side by side.

A chair sings tunes of summer's heat,
As breakfast waits for folks to greet.
Waffles do cartwheels on the plate,
While bacon waits, it can’t be late!

The world wakes up with silly cheer,
With little hopes and much more beer.
So come and join this lively spree,
Where laughter’s free and all are glee!

Worlds Awakened in Gentle Starlight

A moonlit cat plays tag with night,
Chasing shadows with delight.
Stars snicker, twinkling down below,
While owls in top hats steal the show.

The crickets recite bedtime tales,
Of feathered ships with dragon sails.
While sleepy bugs sip nectar tea,
Underneath the grand, sway tree.

A goldfish dreams of flying high,
Despite the bowl where bubbles lie.
Each splash brings forth a witty sigh,
As fireflies blink a cheeky bye.

From twilight grows a canvas bright,
Where laughter begs for gentle light.
So twirl and toss your woes away,
In this wild night where we can play!

A Canvas of Shimmering Potential

In the morning’s early glow,
Pajamas dance with joy, oh so slow.
The coffee pot laughs with a ring,
As it brews the magic of everything.

Plates of pancakes take a leap,
With syrup rivers running deep.
Butterflies play hopscotch on toast,
While the toaster grins and brags the most.

In a garden where socks start to bloom,
And daisies shout in their colorful room.
Every petal's a cheeky face,
Challenging bees in a grand race.

As sunbeams paint a silly scene,
And laughter keeps rolling like jelly bean.
So fill your heart and lift your eyes,
For life’s a canvas, full of surprise!

Celestial Hues Between Reality and Dream

Where jelly beans rain from the sky,
A unicorn waves, oh so spry.
With puppet clouds that bounce above,
Kites made of laughter, wrapped in love.

The grass tickles toes, oh so bold,
As whispers of giggles weave tales told.
And shadows wear hats, quite absurd,
While squirrels compose a silly word.

A trampoline moon does flips with glee,
Bouncing dreams for you and me.
While stars play hide and seek, so bright,
Chasing dreams that dance in the night.

So let your heart skip, jump, and run,
With every ray of morning sun.
Hints of mischief wrapped in beams,
In this world of whimsical dreams!

Paintings of Light and Lullabies

Morning paints the world so bright,
Colors dancing, pure delight.
Squirrels giggle with acorn hats,
While birds engage in silly chats.

Sunbeams drench a sleepy bee,
Buzzing 'round with wildlery.
A butterfly takes a wobbly flight,
In a chase with shadows, oh what a sight!

Puddle jumping, girls in glee,
Splashing water, oh me, oh me!
The sun blinks, it's gone too soon,
Leaving us to whistle a tune.

Lullabies woven in the air,
Crickets laughing without a care.
Night spins tales, a gentle tease,
As dreams settle in, oh what a breeze!

Kisses from the Fading Stars

Stars wink down in playful jest,
Whisper secrets; we're guests.
Moonbeams tease the sleepy town,
While shadows wear a silken gown.

Laughter wraps around the night,
Bats perform their aerial flight.
Jellybeans fall from a sky so wide,
A sugary ride toward the tide.

Cosmic kittens in a twinkle race,
Stealing dreams, a friendly chase.
Galaxies chuckle with a swirl,
As wishes dance and giggles twirl.

When sun rises, giggles fade,
But memories of moonlight played.
Kisses linger in the breeze,
As morning yawns and stretch with ease.

Nebulas of Quiet Possibility

Clouds puff up in hats so grand,
As rainbanks spring in fairyland.
Marshmallow dreams float up so high,
Candy sprinkle the evening sky.

Worms giggle in the soft, wet ground,
Telling jokes without a sound.
Bubbles rise, a frothy cheer,
Frogs croak loudly, lend an ear!

Silly whispers in the air,
Grasshoppers leap without a care.
Every blade a story spins,
Of playful mishaps and silly wins.

Stars above wink at the show,
Kites tangled in a breezy flow.
With every laugh, the world reclaims,
The joy of dreams, the folly of names.

Visions Beyond the Gossamer Veil

A curtain made of laughter falls,
Breezes tickle through the halls.
Butterflies wear shoes too tight,
Dancing in the glimmering light.

Pixies play with twinkling dust,
While puzzled ants break off to rest.
A flower yawns with morning tea,
As day blends in with joyful glee.

Lemon drops tumble from the trees,
As squirrels conspire with the bees.
Gossamer threads weave a silly tale,
Of moonlit dances without fail.

So giggles ride on wispy dreams,
In fields of colors and sunlit beams.
Each moment whispers a little song,
In the joyous air where we belong.

Chasing Shadows of Fleeting Moments

In the garden, giggles bloom,
The sun's a prankster in full plume.
A bumblebee steals my hat,
And off it flies, imagine that!

Silly squirrels dance on trees,
As if they're twirling in the breeze.
A shadow stretches, jumps and skips,
It seems to mimic all my quips.

Butterflies flaunt their hues so bright,
Chasing them feels purely right.
I turned around to find a friend,
But all I found was my loose end.

The sun dips low, the shadows blend,
A playful riddle, without end.
In every corner, laughter springs,
In this mad world, the joy it brings.

Radiance in the Wake of Slumber

Woke up late, my socks don't match,
A wonder why my hair's a scratch.
The toast pops up, it seems to leap,
A daring feat, my mouth now cheap!

Giggles echo in the morn,
My cat just wore a twig as horn.
The milk spills out, a comic scene,
It seems my breakfast loves routine!

Jumping jacks in pajamas worn,
My coffee's gone, my tongue now torn.
I spill some juice, it starts to run,
This life's a race, and I've just begun!

So watch the sun, it's shining wide,
Embrace the chaos, let it slide.
With every slip and awkward twist,
Life dances on, a playful twist.

Serendipity in Glimmers of Light

A shimmer here, a sparkle there,
I tripped on air and found a bear!
Not really, just a fluffy toy,
It gave a wink and brought me joy.

Sunbeams bounce off my breakfast bowl,
While jelly rolls, that is my goal.
I snagged a kiss from a silly spoon,
And now I’m dancing like a loon!

Serendipitous spills accrue,
My tea’s a rainbow, oh how it grew!
Each moment’s funny, each laugh a cheer,
If I slip again, I’ll raise a beer!

The light does glimmer, shadows play,
In this absurd comedy ballet.
With laughter wrapped around my heart,
Every misstep’s a work of art.

Ethereal Mornings in Stillness

The dawn arrives, a laugh so bright,
My sleepy face is quite a sight.
With mismatched slippers, I take a stroll,
Coffee dreams ascend toward the bowl.

Birds perform their morning song,
They chirp and dance, that's where they belong.
A breeze rolls in, it tickles my nose,
A giggling gig, in frosty clothes!

A cat casually claims the sun,
While I misplace my cup—it's fun!
Each quiet moment punctured with cheer,
In this blissful haze, the absurd is near.

As night creeps back to steal the day,
I'll laugh again, in my own way.
These mornings may seem odd, it's true,
But who needs normal when weird's the view?

Glistening Tales of the Unseen

A tiny bead on grass does dance,
As ants march by, they miss the chance.
"Excuse me, friend!" one shouts in glee,
"You're shining bright, let's have some tea!"

But splashing tea is quite a feat,
The cups all roll, we laugh, we cheat.
While puddles form, we sit and giggle,
They slide on leaves, it starts a wiggle.

The sun peeks through, mischievous light,
Adds glint and sparkle, oh what a sight!
The tales of droplets make us snort,
While squirrels join in, it's quite the sport.

So here we sit, in this bright haze,
With wild stories, lost in a maze.
A splash, a laugh, then off we roll,
In this wet world, we find our soul.

Whispers of Morning Mist

A fog rolls in, it wears a grin,
The trees are chuckling, where to begin?
Little whispers float on high,
While flowers giggle, oh my, oh my!

A bunny hops, with quite a flair,
It trips on dew, flies through the air!
It lands on leaves, they laugh with glee,
"Join the fun, come bounce with me!"

The clouds above play peek-a-boo,
While sunlight's rays dance, bright and blue.
Each misty puff becomes our friend,
In this odd shindig, there's no end.

So as we frolic, let joy unfurl,
With silly antics, around we twirl.
In morning's haze, we find delight,
With giggles sprouting, pure and light.

Shimmering Echoes of Dawn

The morning breaks with sparkly tunes,
While sleepy stars retreat till noon.
A rooster crows, a bit off-key,
The cats all laugh, they’re loud with glee.

Umbrellas open, then close with flair,
A gust of wind flies everywhere!
Socks become hats, oh what a sight,
With giggling friends, it feels just right.

A random splash, a fishy cheer,
It wiggles up, and disappears!
The splash it makes, it sparks a dream,
We all erupt in fits and scream.

So come ye all, with humor bright,
We’ll chase the sun till evening’s light.
With shimmering echoes, we’ll sing along,
In this silly world, we all belong.

Glistening Thoughts in Silver Light

A moonbeam teases, with playful grace,
It tickles trees, and lights up space.
The shadows chuckle, hang loose and wide,
Join in the fun, let's take a ride!

A city cat prances, tail held high,
It somersaults, and then jumps shy.
A dog might chase, a squirrel too,
As giggles bounce, like morning dew.

Reflective puddles show sweet surprise,
With faces and jokes that make us rise.
A quacking duck joins in the race,
We're all a mess, but full of grace.

So in this silver, glistening glow,
We twirl and leap, a silly show.
With laughter blooming, hearts so bright,
Our thoughts take flight in the soft night.

Petals in the Gentle Breeze

Fluffy clouds like marshmallows fly,
While flowers giggle as they wave bye.
A bee in a tux, so keen on a snack,
Twirls with a laugh, then buzzes right back.

The sun yawns wide, and hiccups with glee,
As grass tickles toes, oh so playfully.
Squirrels in bowties begin their parade,
With acorns in pockets, their silly charade.

A cat on a lily pad strikes quite the pose,
Planning grand schemes with her wet little nose.
A wind chime chuckles, its jingles so bright,
While frogs in the pond host a dance every night.

When petals start swirling in soft, merry flings,
Nature announces that joy always sings.
So come join the party, grab your best hat,
Where fun and laughter make silly antics at that!

Echoes of Soft Awakening

In the morning, the toast sings a tune,
While socks play hide-and-seek ‘til the noon.
A cat sporting slippers offers a grin,
As coffee does pirouettes, trying to win.

Chirpy birds gossip in trees, quite bemused,
While the sun flips pancakes, so bright and enthused.
Every shadow chuckles, a playful disguise,
As silliness dances in blinks of the eyes.

The toaster pops up with a jubilant cheer,
Inviting the muffins to come join right here.
A fly in a top hat performs a grand show,
As cereal dives in, all set to flow.

The light through the window winks sweetly and bold,
As breakfast conspiracies quietly unfold.
So raise up your spoon in this comedic feast,
Where laughter and joy are never released!

Glimmers of Sleepy Reverie

A sleepyhead yawns, with dreams on his mind,
As pillow bears stories, amusingly blind.
A bear dances gently, twirling in night,
While stars giggle softly, their twinkles delight.

Blankets conspire with mischievous schemes,
Finding the best of enchanted night dreams.
A rubber duck dives into waves of a snooze,
While shadows perform, dressed in whimsical hues.

Lamps huddle close, whispering secrets of light,
A sock takes a bow, it’s quite the sight!
The moon paints the ceiling with glimmers and cheer,
As slumbering jesters make mischief appear.

So float on these giggles, let dreams take their flight,
In the carnival night where the sillies ignite.
With a wink from the stars, it's a party so bright,
As laughter takes stage in the heart of the night!

Chasing Elusive Horizons

The horizon beckons with a cheeky grin,
As clouds wear pajamas in marvelous spin.
A rabbit in shades lounges under a tree,
Forgetting his chores, sipping carrot iced tea.

A snail with a backpack plots out his quest,
While ants in a choir sing songs of the best.
The sun hitches rides on the back of a kite,
As wind does a jig, full of giggles and light.

With every new dawn, it’s a game of surprise,
Where shadows play tag under brightening skies.
The daisies all chuckle, with petals that sway,
Encouraging dreams to come out and play.

So chase those horizons, they bounce and they tease,
With laughter like bubbles carried by breeze.
Join the grand frolic, don’t miss out the show,
Where fun is the treasure, and joy’s always in tow!

Floating Wisps of Thoughtful Wanderings

In a land where socks just wander free,
A giraffe plays chess with a buzzing bee.
Clouds take breaks, sipping on rain,
While thoughts play tag, never in vain.

Fish wear hats and dance in rows,
Chasing their tails where the river flows.
Each leaf giggles as it begins to sway,
In this silly realm where the sun likes to play.

Worms read novels beneath the soil,
While ants debate the merits of toil.
The clock dances, always a beat ahead,
As puddles hold secrets we've never read.

So grab your hat, let your wishes soar,
In the garden of thoughts, there's always more.
Where humor blooms in every nook,
And ponderings dance like a storybook.

Trails of Light in Enchanted Gardens

Butterflies wear glasses, oh what a sight,
Debating the merits of day and night.
Rabbits on scooters race for the prize,
While daisies chat, sharing sweet lies.

A snail sits pondering life's vibrant hues,
While crickets offer their nightly news.
The moon's a jester, playing tricks with stars,
In this wild place where laughter is ours.

Squirrels juggle acorns, trying to impress,
While waterfalls gossip in silken dress.
The wind whispers secrets, both funny and wise,
Tickling the leaves under brightening skies.

So let your heart skip, unleash your delight,
In a world where whimsy dances in light.
With every petal, a giggle unfolds,
In these garden trails, where magic beholds.

Blushing Petals of Early Light

Morning giggles spark across the lawn,
As sleepy flowers yawn and stretch, then dawn.
Sunbeams slip in, tickle the flowers,
While ladybugs plan their counting hours.

A bumblebee buzzes, hats on all sides,
He chats with a worm about butterfly strides.
Caterpillars knit with threads of the sun,
Saying, 'This life is just too much fun!'

Grass blades chatter, sharing tales from night,
While shadows play hide and seek in the light.
Every petal blushes with laughter's embrace,
In this cheeky bloom of nature's own grace.

Join in the frolic, let your heart shine,
In gardens of giggles and sips of sweet wine.
For laughter in petals is always near,
In the daylight's embrace, there's nothing to fear.

Melodies of a Softly Waking World

A rooster sings in a tutu and crown,
In a world where the grass wears a frown.
The sunrise winks, all golden and bright,
With a mischievous pulse in the morning light.

Squirrels strum ukuleles, oh what a tune!
While sunflowers snap their fingers at noon.
The breeze carries whispers of silly delights,
As the world wakes up, it giggles and bites.

The puddles reflect tiny birds with flair,
As clouds toss jokes on the morning air.
Harmony hums from the rustling trees,
Tickling the roots, teasing the bees.

So dance with the laughter, tread soft on the ground,
In this world of whimsy, joy can be found.
With melodies playing through every hour,
Waking dreams blossom, enchanting with power.

Veils of Light and Illusion

In the garden, giggles spin,
With sunbeams dancing on my chin.
The flowers whisper silly tunes,
While bees hum like cartoon raccoons.

A butterfly, in polka dots,
Lost track of all its sunny thoughts.
It dodges clouds like dodgy friends,
And flutters where the laughter bends.

The spider weaves with thread so fine,
Tales of socks lost at the vine.
Each droplet like a crystal tear,
But really, just a kid's new beer.

In the sky, the clouds pretend,
To be my long-lost fishing friend.
As rainbows play like silly fools,
While birds all mimic in their schools.

Morning's Embrace in Luminous Silence

The sun sneezed gold upon my face,
A radiant flare of sunny grace.
I giggled as the shadows raced,
Like clumsy dancers in a chase.

My toast popped up with such a cheer,
It jumped like it had no fear.
A squirrel stole my morning snack,
And laughed when I gave him a whack.

The kettle whistled jazz so sweet,
Reminding me I missed my seat.
I danced around, avoiding chores,
As socks and slippers joined in scores.

The world awoke in fits of glee,
The curtains waved to tease the spree.
With morning's light, the fun begins,
As shadows peek, and laughter wins.

Fluttering Leaves of Thoughtful Winds

The breeze is tickling leafy hair,
As autumn's shoes return to wear.
The trees complain, oh what a fuss,
As leaves rain down, they call the bus.

A squirrel dons a tiny hat,
And darts around to chase the cat.
They play a game of hide and seek,
While nature giggles, loud and cheek.

A gust blows by, the leaves take flight,
In swirling dances, pure delight.
Each branch sways with a playful grin,
As whispers swirl, let fun begin.

The clouds above share silly jokes,
While laughter lives among the oaks.
In every rustle, merry sound,
A treasure trove of joy is found.

A Symphony of Hazy Halos

A hazy sun peeked through the play,
Where butterflies led bright ballet.
The world turned into a cartoon,
With giggles spilling like a tune.

A cat in shades reclined so proud,
Its sleepy grin spoke to the crowd.
With rodents joining in the fun,
Their paws cha-cha 'til day is done.

The flowers yawned with colors bold,
Each petal wrapped in tales untold.
As ants played drums upon the ground,
A melody of mischief found.

In every corner, joy gleams bright,
As shadows dance with morning light.
The air's alive with laughter's tone,
Where hazy dreams have proudly grown.

Traces of Wonder in Waking Light

A snail once dreamed of a marathon run,
He trained on leaves, thought it was fun.
But when the race day came with great flair,
He crawled two inches, and stopped for a dare.

The sun stretched out, yawning wide,
A squirrel on a swing tried to glide.
He missed the branch, and fell with a thud,
Landing in a pile of sticky mud.

The flowers giggled in morning time,
As bumblebees buzzed their silly rhyme.
A ladybug laughed at a grasshopper's joke,
While the ladybug danced, a butterfly strode.

As clouds danced by in a fluffy parade,
The shadows all juggled in bright masquerade.
A turtle lost track of his shell on the run,
But laughed when he found it—a slow-motion stun.

Chasing Glimmers of Fleeting Inspiration

A cat in a hat thought he'd be the king,
He practiced his meow, it was quite the thing.
But in front of the mirror, he tripped on his tail,
And ended the show doing a cartwheel fail.

An ant with ambitions to start a new look,
Wore shades and a scarf—oh what a hook!
But slipping on crumbs from a picnic spread,
He ended up buried—now where's my bread?

The moon missed its cue, slipped down a small hill,
Chasing away shadows with a laugh and a thrill.
Stars giggled down, as they lit up the night,
While the clouds whispered secrets in pure delight.

With pencils and paint made of giggles and cheer,
Colors spilled laughter for all who came near.
A rabbit in slippers danced through the lane,
And discovered that hopping is never a pain.

Shades of Whimsy in Daily Life

A chicken tried flying, just once, to be cool,
She fluttered and flapped, looking quite the fool.
With a cluck and a squawk, she gave it a go,
And landed in compost with a scrumptious 'whoa!'

Each morning the toaster would pop with a grin,
While the bread would jump-dance as if it could win.
The butter would slide right down in a race,
Oh what a breakfast with laughter to chase!

A goldfish on skates could not find its way,
It rolled in a bubble and danced all day.
The cat in the corner just watched with delight,
As the fish twirled around, a jazzy fish flight.

On swings of imagination, we fly and we sway,
A parade of odd creatures brings smiles every day.
In funny little moments, the world feels alive,
With giggles and wiggles, our spirits will thrive.

Morning's Light and the Heart's Lullaby

The rooster's alarm clock was out on a spree,
He crowed like a rock star, a true VIP.
While the lazy old dog just rolled in the sun,
With dreams of some bacon—oh, wasn't that fun?

A pancake flipped high with a flourish so bold,
Did a spin in the air, as the syrup retold
A tale of a breakfast that couldn't sit still,
And landed right squishy on top of a hill.

The sun played hide-and-seek, peeking through trees,
While squirrels munched nuts, with giggles in the breeze.
A rabbit wore glasses, a book in its paw,
Reading tales of adventure with a snort and a jaw.

With laughter around, the morning began,
Each creature a player in day's little plan.
In the heart of the light, where whimsy does bow,
We find simple joys and a wink from a cow.

Radiant Trails of Chasing Dreams

Tiny sprites dance in the morn's glow,
With giggles that sprinkle where wildflowers grow.
They tease the clouds, a feathered caper,
As sunbeams waltz, the world's a paper.

The squirrels are judges, they nod with delight,
While bumblebees buzz in their jolly flight.
A parade of mishaps, they stumble and roll,
On this whimsical path, they play their role.

Frogs in tuxedos croak out a tune,
While worms do the limbo beneath the moon.
With each little hop and each funny fall,
Nature's a circus, we're all at the ball.

So chase your laughs like you chase the breeze,
With twinkling eyes that are sure to tease.
For life's a giggle, a joyous scheme,
In radiant trails, we chase our dream.

Mystic Lightborne upon Awakening

A sleepy sun yawns from behind the hills,
As birds wear crowns of their morning thrills.
With coffee clouds brewing in the sky,
Dreams ride on whispers, the time to fly!

The toast sings pop tunes from its golden throne,
While socks play peekaboo, the floors are their zone.
A cat on the window sill, drowsy yet spry,
Chasing invisible mice that zoom by.

In this cozy chaos, joy finds its way,
With laughter and wiggles that greet the day.
For in this light, magic braids the scene,
Making even the grumpy turn gleefully keen.

So let's skip through shadows, tickle the sun,
And trample the weeds just to have some fun.
With whimsies a-plenty in morning's tune,
We'll dance with delight, a magical boon.

Reflections of Joy in a Sunlit Stream

Rivers of giggles flow under the trees,
Where fish wear tiny glasses and swim with ease.
They splash like the children who dip their toes,
As laughter cascades where the bubblegum flows.

The dragonflies sparkle like stars on a spree,
Whispering secrets to those who can see.
While turtles in sun hats debate fashion flair,
A picnic of nonsense floats sweet in the air.

With sandwiches wiggling and chips that can dance,
Each bite brings a grin, a joyous chance.
So gather your pals by the water's gleam,
And dip into laughter – the perfect theme.

In this stream of smiles, reflections abound,
Where all of our crazies are joyfully found.
Let your worries drift like leaves on a beam,
And splash in the moments that make our hearts dream.

Wandering Thoughts in a Sea of Dazzle

Fluffy clouds wearing hats wander the blue,
On their quest for marshmallows, drifting like dew.
Gigantic ice cream cones sway in the breeze,
Calling all wanderers, come taste the freeze!

In fields of confetti and rainbow delight,
A parade of oddities twirls into sight.
With whirligigs whizzing, and laughter that soars,
Each moment's a treasure that joyously roars.

The sun winks with mischief, it scatters the light,
On the dance floor of daisies, all giddy and bright.
A tuba-playing snail leads a merry band,
While squirrels juggle acorns, oh isn't it grand?

So lose yourself thrilling in whimsical charms,
Where wandering thoughts cradle you in their arms.
With giggles as lifeboats and whimsy as sails,
We float in a dazzle, where laughter prevails.

Hidden Paths of Radiance and Thought

In the morning's gentle glow,
A squirrel wears a tiny hat.
It dances round, a funny show,
Chasing shadows, oh, imagine that!

Through the grass, a giggle slips,
As butterflies do cartwheels wide.
A ladybug takes funny trips,
On a leaf, in laughter, they glide.

Puddles hold reflective pools,
With frogs that sing in silly tones.
They croak their quirky little rules,
Riding bubbles, far from homes.

In this world of silly sights,
Each corner hides a playful jest.
With chuckles shared from day to nights,
We all become a welcome guest.

Dancers in the Light of New Horizons

Sunbeams twirl on morning grass,
While ants wear shoes made out of clay.
They prance along, they never pass,
A chance to dance—I dare to say!

A bumblebee hums tunes so sweet,
Wearing headphones, buzzing loud.
With every step, they skip a beat,
Creating smiles in the crowd.

Clouds above, a fluffy stage,
With raindrops plummeting in glee.
Each droplet writes its comic page,
Painting laughter, wild and free.

While shadows stretch, the sun stands tall,
In this comedy, we all belong.
With every stumble, rise with a sprawl,
Join the dance, let's laugh along!

The Universe's Canvas at First Light

As morning spills its gold so bright,
The stars decide to take a nap.
A comet trips, oh what a sight,
And lands upon a cosmic map!

Nearby, the planets play charades,
While asteroids throw cosmic pies.
With laughter ringing through their blades,
They craft a space team—what a prize!

The sun, a painter, spreads its hues,
But forgot his brush—it's quite obscene.
He flings out orange, pink, and blues,
With specks of green across the scene.

In this vast, imaginative realm,
The cosmos bursts with silly schemes.
Here, giggles flourish at the helm,
As laughter blooms within our dreams.

Twilight Whispers of Untold Stories

As twilight twinkles, shadows grow,
A cat dons glasses, reading tales.
His whiskers twitch, oh what a show,
In magic realms where nothing fails.

The moon, a jester in the night,
Juggles stars like popcorn balls.
They giggle, shimmering with delight,
As echoes of joy through twilight calls.

Fireflies buzz a dance of sparks,
As crickets chirp their nightly tunes.
In this symphony, laughter parks,
While owls wear hats, not just balloons.

Each hidden story in the dark,
Is filled with chuckles, sly and quaint.
In the tales of night, we embark,
As dreams take flight without restraint.

Celestial Whispers at the Break of Day

The sun yawns wide, a sleepy face,
Tickling the clouds, in warm embrace.
Stars giggle, hiding from the light,
While birds argue ‘bout their flight.

A pancake plops, the skillet sings,
Butter dances with the morning's flings.
Squirrels cavort in a nutty spree,
While I chuckle with my cup of tea.

The moon waves bye, a jester's grin,
As shadows stretch, they wave back in.
A dog chases after a runaway shoe,
How the world smiles, what a view!

With laughter ringing, I step outside,
Seeking mischief, my heart is wide.
In each blooming flower, the laughter thrives,
As morning awakens, oh how it jives!

A Dance of Light Across the Earth

Sunbeams slide like a playful cat,
Chasing the shadows where they sat.
Grass whispers secrets to the breeze,
While ants hold court beneath the trees.

A butterfly fluffs its polka-dot wings,
As squirrels impersonate kings and queens.
Laughter erupts from a butterfly's kiss,
Each petal's giggle, not one to miss.

The daisies sway, their jig is grand,
An orchestra hiding in the land.
Here comes a worm with a party hat,
Caterpillars cheer, 'We love that!'

Bubbles float in the air, so free,
What a mess for a honeybee!
Laughter bounces in the sunlight's gleam,
A silly world, straight from a dream.

Elysian Fields of Softest Brightness

Clouds play hopscotch in the sky,
An apple rolls and decides to fly.
Flowers swap jokes, petals unfold,
While the sun spills warmth like stories told.

A frog croaks loudly, stealing the show,
Acrobatic ants put on a flow.
With twirls and twirls, they dance with flair,
As butterflies float, without a care.

Blades of grass wear dew like crowns,
While giggles echo through the towns.
Caterpillars in tuxedos skip,
Joining in on a whimsical trip.

The wind herds clouds like silly sheep,
While daylight nudges everyone to leap.
The world giggles in colors bright,
With laughter painted across the light.

Murmurs of a Sunlit Reverie

A squirrel wears sunglasses, what a sight,
Dancing on branches, just pure delight.
A rooster croons in a disco tone,
As flowers wave, in shades well-known.

Clouds toss confetti from high above,
While bees unite to find their love.
A rabbit hops with a jaunty flair,
Doing the cha-cha in the bright air.

Sunbeams set the grass ablaze,
As fireflies blink in whimsical ways.
A frog with sass sings a winning tune,
Tapping its toes beneath the moon.

Each moment bursts with giggly cheer,
In this land where silliness is dear.
With dreams that dance on each spark of light,
The world twirls with glee, oh what a sight!

Gold-kissed Finery at Day's Break

In the garden, sunlight spills,
A cat trips over daffodil thrills.
The bee wears a hat, proud and bright,
Buzzing around in morning light.

Giggling grass blades sway with ease,
Tickling the toes of dancing bees.
A squirrel juggles acorns with flair,
As if the world has no weight to bear.

Pigeons strut in neatly pressed suits,
While ants hold a party in little boots.
A frog leaps up, steals the show,
Singing a tune with a croaky glow.

Morning grins in a cornflower blue,
As laughter and mischief twinkle anew.
The sun gives a wink, a cheeky tease,
Inviting us all to play among the trees.

Fleeting Whispers of the Awakening

Sleepy whispers in the air,
A rabbit's nose twitches with flair.
A rooster who forgot the song,
Makes morning feel delightfully wrong.

Clouds wear pajamas, white and fluffy,
While butterflies flaunt in colors zesty.
A puppy chases its own tail,
As sunshine blooms and giggles prevail.

Coffee spills—oh, what a scene!
The cup's now twirling like a queen.
Laughing squirrels crash the fair,
With nutty jokes they love to share.

Day awakens with a funny lurch,
While shadows dance and brightly perch.
Every moment holds a spark,
As laughter bubbles in the park.

Threads of Illumination and Wonder

The sun knits a sweater of gold,
While a snail tells tales, quite bold.
A ladybug flips like a pro,
On threads of light, it steals the show.

Wakeful daisies burst with cheer,
Winking at bumblebees, come near.
An owl who missed the night's big spree,
Realizes the day is not for he!

A frog fancies itself a knight,
Frolicking 'round with leafy might.
He's got a sheathed acorn sword,
In a kingdom of laughter, never bored.

Dance, flutter, the giggles arise,
As sunbeams come from joyous skies.
Every moment blooms and spins,
In threads of light that bring the grins.

Glimmers of Enchantment at Sunrise

The dawn rolls in with playful flair,
A sleepy crow forgets to stare.
Chasing shadows, the colors run,
As daisies wink at the giggling sun.

A bee does ballet on a petal's tip,
While a butterfly takes a joyful dip.
Puppy breath catches the morning breeze,
But only snores come from the trees.

A raccoon in pajamas, quite the sight,
Raiding picnic plans in broad daylight.
He sips from what seems a teacup fine,
Delighted in mischief, oh how he shines!

Laughter rings as the day awakes,
Shiny moments that joyfully quakes.
In the whimsical dance of the new,
Every giggle is magic and true.

Secrets Traced in Unseen Air

Tiny gems on leaves reside,
A squirrel wonders, eyes open wide.
Did someone spill a jar of sparkles?
Or is it just my funny goggles?

A breeze tickles my funny bone,
Whispers secrets not yet known.
Are those raindrops or ants in a race?
I can't quite keep up with this pace!

Laughter dances on sunbeams bright,
Nature plays hide and seek in white.
A giggle floats from flower to tree,
Are they laughing at you or me?

In every nook, pure mischief hides,
Like tiny pirates on joyful rides.
Chasing whimsy in morning light,
Who knew daybreak could ignite delight?

Reverie Born of Gentle Radiance

A butterfly checks its reflection,
Is it a bird? Oh, what a deception!
With painted wings like a funny bow,
It flutters past, putting on a show.

Sunbeams play on a puddle's face,
I leap and splash! What a silly chase!
Will this splash bring forth a cheer?
Or will I just end up wet, oh dear?

A cat with shades and a top hat too,
Struts along, as if it knew.
"Where's my breakfast?" it seems to say,
With all this charm, who could delay?

The morning whispers silly tunes,
As flowers dance under big cartoons.
I twirl with joy to greet the fun,
Life's a joke, and I'm not done!

Enigmatic Light Woven into Dawn

Light weaves tales with a wink and grin,
Playing tricks where the dreams begin.
Is that a lightbulb or just a star?
Hope they don't mind my close-up bazaar!

The sun pokes fun through the leafy screen,
Peeking in on my silly routine.
A dance party breaks out with glee,
Who brought the snacks? Was it me?

Ghosts of shadows move in a jig,
Hiding behind a garden twig.
They pull a prank, but I see clear,
Just an orange bouncing near here.

So as the world wakes with a sigh,
I laugh and wave to the shy blue sky.
For in this glow, there's fun to find,
A riddle of light, forever entwined.

Fragrant Memories in Morning’s Breath

The air is sweet with a cupcake's scent,
But alas, it’s just breakfast, I lament.
A pastry thief in my daydreams strolls,
While I munch on cereal—lost in my goals.

Pancakes stack like a wobbly tower,
“Can you eat me?” they softly cower.
Bacon giggles from the frying pan,
This breakfast orchestra's quite the band!

The toast pops up with startling flair,
“Save me a crumb if you truly care!”
Each bite I take is a funny cheer,
What’s more delightful than food right here?

Morning laughs roll like fluffy clouds,
As I dive headfirst into playful crowds.
With memories sweet, I step ahead,
To a day where laughter is our bread.

www.ingramcontent.com/pod-product-compliance
Lightning Source LLC
Chambersburg PA
CBHW051628160426
43209CB00004B/564
9781805666172